Hip HAMSTER Projects

*Lots of cool craft
projects inside*

Isabel Thomas

heinemann
raintree

© 2016 Heinemann-Raintree
an imprint of Capstone Global Library, LLC
Chicago, Illinois

To contact Capstone Global Library please call 800-747-4992, or visit our web site www.capstonepub.com

Edited by Helen Cox Cannons and Holly Beaumont
Designed by Philippa Jenkins
Picture research by Tracy Cummins
Production by Helen McCreath
Originated by Capstone Global Library Ltd
Printed and bound in China

19 18 17 16 15
10 9 8 7 6 5 4 3 2 1

Library of Congress Cataloging-in-Publication Data
Cataloging-in-publication data is available at the Library of Congress.
ISBN 978-1-4109-8067-0 (hardback)
ISBN 978-1-4109-8082-3 (ebook PDF)

Acknowledgments
We would like to thank the following for permission to reproduce photographs:
Alamy: imageBROKER, 12; Getty Images: Todd Sappington, Cover Bottom Left; Shutterstock: Brooke Whatnall, Design Element, Elya Vatel, 17 Bottom Right, 28 Bottom Left, George M Photography, 28 (hat), Igor Kovalchuk, 1, Multiple Use, Jagodka, 22 (hamster), SeDmi, 18 Top Left.

All other photography by Capstone Studio: Karon Dubke.

007365LEOF15

Safety instructions for adult helper

Some of the projects in this book involve steps that should only be carried out by an adult—these are indicated in the text. Always follow the instructions carefully.

ADULT HELP

Contents

Look for the paw-print icons. These tell you how long each project will take.

 = up to 30 minutes

 = up to 1 hour

 = more than 1 hour

Hung Up on Hamsters!

If you're hung up on hamsters, you'll love the projects in this book. If you are lucky enough to have a hamster yourself, or just love those cute cheeks, there is so much to make and do.

- ❂ Make gifts for friends or relatives.
- ❂ Decorate your bedroom with hamster designs.
- ❂ Create homemade hamster treats and toys.
- ❂ Throw a hamster-themed party!

At the back of the book, you'll find a link to a web page packed with templates to use in the projects, and tips on how to use them to create designs of your own!

Getting started

Before starting each project, read the instructions carefully and make sure you have everything you need. Find out if you will need an adult to help with any of the steps. If you are planning to reuse or recycle an object, or decorate walls, clothes, or furniture, check that it's OK first.

nibblesome notecards page 11

pocket hamster page 6

hamster pops page 26

Pet view

Look out for my tips on hamster care as you scamper through the book!

Working safely

Work in an area where you can make a mess, using newspaper to protect the table or floor. Make sure you open the windows or work outside if you are using paint or glue. Keep pets away while you are crafting. Never use paint or glue near a pet—the fumes can be dangerous for animals.

Things...to keep in your craft kit

- Scissors, pens, pencils, paints, paintbrush, ruler, sticky tape, and white glue.

- Pretty found objects such as feathers, stones, and buttons.

- Scraps of pretty fabric, paper, cardboard, newspapers, and magazines.

- Boxes, jars, and containers with interesting shapes (wash and dry food containers before storing them).

- Sewing materials such as a needle and thread, yarn, ribbons, and trimmings.

Fabric Crafts

Sadly, you can't take your hamster to school with you. But you can take these cute crafts!

Pocket hamster

Turn scraps of fabric into a portable pet that is small enough to put in your pencil case.

1 Find the pocket hamster template on the web site (see page 31), print it, and cut it out. Pin the template onto the fabric and cut out matching shapes in felt or furry fabric and white or cream fabric.

2 Stack the two pieces of fabric together (with the furry sides facing in). Sew around the outside of the shapes, leaving a gap at the tail end.

3 Knot the thread and turn the shape inside out.

4 Make a funnel from cardboard and use it to help you fill the fabric shape with rice or beans. Stop before the hamster is full. Sew up the opening tightly.

You will need:

- tracing paper, pencil, and scissors
- felt or furry fabric
- white or cream fabric
- cardboard
- needle and thread
- uncooked rice or dried beans
- three small beads

5 Sew the beads on to make the nose and eyes. Using the project templates, cut two ears from the leftover white or cream fabric and sew them in place. Add whiskers by sewing four long loops of thread around the nose bead and cutting through the loops.

Your fluffy friend can double as a pincushion for sewing projects!

Pet view

I like to rest and sleep during the day, so please only handle me in the evenings, when I'm already awake. I don't like bright lights or loud noises.

TOP TIP

Sprinkle in some dried lavender to make a hamster that smells as nice as it looks!

Super-soft pictures

Create a cross-stitch hamster that's as stroke-able as the real thing!

1 Start by printing a photograph of your hamster onto graph paper. Alternatively, draw a hamster design onto graph paper and color it in.

2 Secure the cross-stitch fabric in an embroidery hoop. Using a pencil, sketch the outline of your design onto it, square by square.

3 Thread the needle with a piece of yarn or thread and knot the end. Starting in one corner of the design, thread the needle up through the canvas so the knot is at the back.

4 Sew over each square with cross-stitch, using the graph paper as a guide. When you need to change color, knot the thread at the back.

You will need:

- graph paper
- pencil or colored pens
- cross-stitch fabric
- embroidery needle
- yarn or embroidery thread in hamstery colors
- embroidery hoop or empty picture frame and thumbtacks
- scissors

An embroidery needle has a large eye and rounded end.

 TOP TIP

If you don't have an embroidery hoop, pinning the fabric to an empty frame will keep it flat while you sew.

Small cross-stitch pictures are perfect for displaying in a key ring or frame.

Pencil pet

Cut two ovals from felt. Glue or sew them together, leaving a ½ inch (1-cm) gap at the large end. Glue or sew on eyes, ears, nose, and whiskers, and simply slip onto a pencil. Why not make a bunch of hamsters in rainbow colors?

TOP TIP

Turn your soft toy into a key ring by sandwiching a loop of ribbon with a key ring attachment between the layers of felt.

Get Crafty with Paper

Uncage your creativity with these hamster-inspired projects.

Just add hamsters!

Do you ever get pretty hamster wrapping paper you can't bear to throw away? Use it to make a hamster-rific pet record book!

1 Cut or tear the magazine or wrapping paper into pieces.

2 Paint a small area of the notebook with diluted glue. Stick on pieces of the paper, overlapping the edges.

3 Repeat until you have covered the notebook with pictures. Leave to dry.

You will need:
- notebook
- old hamster magazines or wrapping paper
- scissors
- diluted white glue (3 parts glue to 1 part water) and brush

Stick the paper on with glue. Brush over a coat of diluted glue to seal your design.

Pet view

Keeping a pet record book will help you to spot if I'm sick or injured. If my eating or sleeping habits change, take your record book along to show the vet.

Nibblesome notecards

A few folds turn a square of paper into something much cuter.

1 Fold the square of paper in half. Then, fold the left third of the rectangle across the middle third.

2 Take the bottom-left corner and fold it back up to the middle. Crease firmly, and then tuck it back in on itself.

3 Next, fold the bottom corner outward to make a paw, and fold the top corner down to make an ear.

4 Finally, fold the top corner backward to make a tail. Add an eye, nose, and whiskers to finish your hamster.

You will need:

- small square of paper
- felt-tip pen

Don't forget to write a secret note inside!

Hamster-rific DIY Projects

It's not just you who needs privacy in a busy house. Help your hamster to hide away during the day, and make your pet feel safe when you handle him or her in the evenings.

Coconut hideaway

Coconut shells make great hamster hideaways. They are just the right size to snuggle up in, and because they are both hard and natural, they are perfect for chewing on.

1 Ask an adult to saw the top off a coconut, about a quarter of the way down. Another option is to put the coconut in a plastic bag and swing it against a wall or floor to break it open. Make sure you do this outside!

2 Use a spoon to scrape the flesh out of the coconut—yum!—then rinse and dry the shell. If there are sharp edges, sand them down, then rinse and dry again.

3 Put the coconut shell into your hamster's home, along with nesting material.

You will need:

- coconut
- spoon
- sandpaper

5 things...to do with a cardboard tube

🐹 Your hamster needs plenty to do inside its cage. Empty paper towel tubes make great ramps, tunnels, and hiding-holes.

🐹 Your hamster loves to gnaw, shred, and chew. This is good for its teeth. Cardboard tubes are easy to replace when they wear down.

🐹 Hide a dry hamster treat inside a soft cardboard tube and fold the ends down. Can your hamster figure out how to get it out?

🐹 Stuff hay inside the tube and position it in the cage as a hay feeder, to stop the hay from mixing with the bedding.

🐹 Try the pencil pot project on page 24.

Pet view

Wild hamsters live underground and never stray too far from their burrows. This is why I'm timid and need plenty of places to hide or snuggle into when it's time for a snooze.

Hamster lanterns

Hamsters are usually only awake in the evening and night. This means the best time to handle hamsters is in the early morning or evening, when they are already awake. The soft light from these pretty lanterns will make your hamster feel at ease and help you bond.

1 Cut or tear the tissue paper into pieces. Include one or two hamster shapes from the templates on the web site (see page 31).

2 Glue the tissue paper shapes onto the outside of the jar, to make pretty patterns.

3 Paint the jar with a coat of diluted glue (1 part glue to 3 parts water).

You will need:

- old jar, washed and dried, label removed
- tissue paper in different colors
- scissors
- white glue and brush

TOP TIP

Light your lanterns with bike lights, glow sticks, or battery-powered tea lights. Never use a candle.

Pet view

It's a bad idea to keep me in your bedroom. I'm only awake at night, so my noisy playing and exercising might keep you awake! Find me a spot that is quiet in the day and where the lights go off at the same time every night.

4 When the glue is dry, your lantern is ready to use. Place a light source inside and screw on the lid.

Turn the main lights off and watch your lantern glow!

Pet pot

It's easy to transfer hamster pictures onto a jar. Just print a design, roll up the paper, and put it inside the jar. Draw or paint over it using a glass pen or paint. This makes a cute holder for a battery-powered tea light or a pretty place to store dry hamster food.

Kitchen Creations

Every hamster loves a treat, but did you know that some store-bought treats have unhealthy ingredients, such as sugar and colorings? Make these delicious alternatives.

Hamster salad bar

Hamsters love leaves such as clover and dandelion, but it's important not to give them plants that grew near a road (which can be dirty) or may have been treated with chemicals (which can be poisonous). Homegrown greens are a great way to safely improve your hamster's daily diet.

1 Cover the bottom of the container with a layer of gravel. Add potting soil until the container is two-thirds full.

2 Water the soil lightly, then plant seeds following the instructions on the packet. Water the seeds, then cover the container with a layer of plastic wrap and keep it in a warm place. Remember to keep the soil damp.

3 Once seedlings have sprouted, move the container to a sunny spot, such as a windowsill, and keep it well watered.

You will need:

- container (flowerpot)
- gravel
- potting soil
- plastic wrap
- seeds of hamster-friendly plants (e.g., dandelion, clover, beansprouts)

Pet view

Give me greens in small amounts to stop me from hiding spare food around my home, which will soon start to rot. Yuck! Some greens, such as rhubarb, potato, and tomato leaves, are poisonous to hamsters, so always check with an expert first.

Hide a cute hamster pebble among the leaves of your hamster salad (see page 18).

Greens keep your hamster healthy.

TOP TIP

Decorate the container to make an extra-pretty pot for your bedroom or kitchen windowsill. You can paint terra-cotta pots using normal poster paint. Ask an adult to brush on a coat of clear varnish afterward, to make the pots waterproof.

Animal Art

Your hamster may not be able to live in your bedroom, but you can fill it with reminders of your BFF—best fluffy friend!

Perfect paperweight

Use fur-toned paint to turn a pebble into a work of art.

You will need:
- large, smooth pebble with a tapered end (the kind you'd find on a beach)
- acrylic paints
- paintbrush
- diluted white glue (3 parts glue to 1 part water)

1 Start by painting your pebble white. When the paint is dry to the touch, brush on tiny strokes of dark-brown paint, then add strokes of lighter paint over it.

2 Paint black eyes, dabbing a tiny dot of white onto each eye to make it gleam (use the end of the brush handle to do this). Add black and pink ears, a pink nose and mouth, and whiskers in white paint.

3 When the paint is dry, carefully brush on a coat of diluted glue to seal your design.

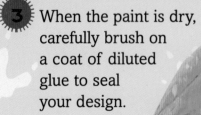

Q Could you ever love a rock?

A Yes, when it looks like a hamster!

Keep out!

This "keep out" sign is just too cute to argue with! Why not make one for your hamster, too? Download the templates (see page 31) and print. Transfer them to a piece of sturdy cardboard and cut them out. Glue them back to back, and decorate each side. On one side, write something like "Come back later, I'm dozing," and on the other side write "Please say hello!"

Hang the ring over your door handle.

Please say hello

Come back later

Bracelet buddy

Use salt dough to make a charming hamster charm.

1. Mix the flour and salt together, then pour in the water slowly, stirring to make a dough. Knead (squeeze and mix) the dough with your hands to make it soft, adding a few more drops of water if you spot any cracks.

2. Roll two small balls of salt dough. Pinch one ball to make the bottom wider than the top. This is your hamster's head.

3. Squish the head onto the body, so the cheeks stick out on the sides. Roll some smaller salt dough balls to add paws, ears, and a belly.

4. Push two beads into the face to make eyes, and another bead to make a nose.

5. Push the eye pin into the top of the hamster's head. Leave the salt dough to dry overnight.

6. When the dough is completely dry, paint your model using acrylic paint. Draw in your hamster's mouth using permanent marker. Add a coat of diluted glue to seal your design.

You will need:

- 1 cup (150 g) flour
- ⅓ cup (75 g) salt
- ¼ cup (60 ml) water
- two small black beads
- eye pin (from a bead store)
- toothpicks
- acrylic paints
- diluted white glue
- permanent marker

Thread your hamster charm onto a bracelet, cell phone, or pencil case.

Hamster cartoons

You can make cute hamster cartoons using fingerprints. Dip a finger in ink and press onto paper. Make prints in different colors. Have fun adding ears, eyes, nose, whiskers, and paws. How many expressions can you give your hamsters?

nervous hamster

happy hamster

shocked hamster

tired hamster

grumpy hamster

TOP TIP

These DIY emoticons are a quick way to personalize cards and invitations.

Upcycle!

Don't throw out old food packaging and containers. Recycle it into awesome accessories for your hamster, and help save the planet at the same time.

Make me a maze

Hamsters need plenty of exercise and they love to explore. This amazing maze will get your hamster's whiskers twitching.

You will need:

- old cardboard packaging without colors or prints
- cardboard tubes (e.g., empty paper towel tubes)
- natural materials such as old coconut shells
- scissors

Make sure everything is empty and clean, with no sharp edges. Remove any plastic parts.

Egg cartons make good hiding places.

1 Use a large cardboard box as a base, cutting the sides down until they are around 12 in. (30 cm) high. This will help you to wedge objects into place without using glue or tape and will stop your hamster from escaping.

2 Make platforms supported by slots in the wall. Hamsters love to stop in spots like these and clean themselves.

3 Slot pieces of cardboard together to make a maze and join several tubes together to make long, branching tunnels. Make some holes smaller than others, so your hamster can enjoy squeezing through.

4 Cut ramps out of cardboard and use a hard-tipped pen to make dents to help your hamster hang on. Having tiny feet has its advantages!

Hide a hamster treat inside for your really smart rodent to track down.

Blocks of wood or thick cardboard can be stacked to make steps.

Pet view

I need plenty of exercise—did you know that hamsters like to run up to 5 miles (8 km) a day? Let me out of my cage every evening to explore. Watch me carefully to make sure I don't escape, and remember that I can chew my way out of a cardboard box!

Pots from packaging

Hamsters can pack a lot of food into their chubby cheeks, which means lots of leftover food packaging. Transform the empty bags into woven pots, for storing your stuff in style.

1. Clean and dry the empty food bags. Cut them up into strips 2 in. (5 cm) wide. You will need four 12-in. (30-cm) strips, and around eight 8-in. (20-cm) strips.

2. Fold each strip over on itself twice, to create stronger strips around ½ in. (1 cm) wide.

3. Cut a circle of cardboard 2 in. (5 cm) wide. This will be the base of your pot. Stick the 12-in. (30-cm) strips across the base in a star pattern, so they are evenly spaced.

4. Turn the base over and fold the strips so they stick straight up into the air. Place an empty cardboard tube on the base, and use a rubber band to hold the strips loosely against the tube. This will be a guide for weaving your pot.

24

5 Take one of the 8-in. (20-cm) strips and tape it to the inside of one of the upright strips. Now weave the strip around the tube, in and out of the upright strips. When you get back to the start, tape the ends of the strip together and trim off any excess.

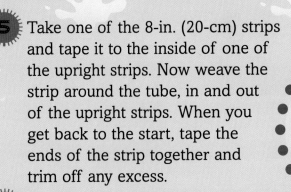

6 Repeat step 5 with the other 8-in. (20-cm) strips, working your way up the tube. When you feel that your pot is high enough, remove the tube. Snip the upright strips so they finish ½ in. (1 cm) above the top of the pot. Then fold them down and glue them in place.

 TOP TIP

Give the whole pot a coat of watered down glue to make it super-strong!

Throw a Hamster Party!

Your pet is part of the family, so celebrate your hamster's birthday with a party in his or her honor.

Hamster pops

These bite-sized cakes are super-cute and definitely super-yummy.

1 Crumble the cake into a mixing bowl to make fine crumbs. Add icing, one spoonful at a time, until the mixture sticks together like dough.

2 Break off small pieces of the dough and roll them into balls. Add two small lumps of dough to each ball to make ears. Put the balls into a refrigerator for an hour. Meanwhile, ask an adult to melt the white chocolate for you.

You will need:

- sponge cake
- buttercream icing
- white chocolate buttons
- wooden or rolled-paper sticks
- pink, heart-shaped sprinkles
- small, edible silver balls
- black writing icing or small amount of melted milk chocolate
- colander (upside down)

Pet view

Remember, cake pops are for people only! Never feed me human treats such as chocolate or cornflakes.

3 When the cake balls are firm, take them out of the refrigerator. Dip each stick into the melted chocolate and push it into the ball.

4 Holding the stick, dip the ball of cake into the melted white chocolate and roll it from side to side, until it is completely covered.

5 Carefully slot the stick into the colander to hold it in place.

6 While the chocolate is still wet, stick on a pink, heart-shaped sprinkle to make a nose and small silver balls to make eyes.

7 Repeat these steps until you have coated every cake ball. Put the cake pops in a cool place.

8 When the chocolate has set, use the writing icing or melted milk chocolate to add a mouth to each one.

The chocolate will help the stick stay in place.

Keep the cake pops in the refrigerator until you are ready to serve them.

27

Make a hamster piñata

A piñata is an exciting party game that is broken open to reveal the treats inside.

1 Blow up the balloons and tie the ends. Tear the newspaper into strips. Mix the glue, flour, and water together to make a thin paste.

2 Dip the newspaper strips into the paste and use them to cover each balloon. Add three layers of newspaper, leaving each layer to dry before adding the next.

3 When the final layer is completely dry, pop the balloons with a pin. Carefully cut the bottom off each balloon, cutting around 2 in. (5 cm) from the ties. Tape the cut ends of the balloons together, to make a figure-eight shape.

4 Cut a small flap at the top of the piñata. This will be where you put in the treats.

You will need:

- two balloons
- 3 oz. (85 ml) white glue
- 1 cup (150 g) plain flour
- 2 cups (500 ml) water
- newspaper
- paintbrush
- pin and scissors
- sticky tape
- glue for decorating
- crepe paper or tissue paper in brown, white, black, and pink
- assorted craft papers
- string

5 Decorate your piñata with colored tissue or crepe paper. To make fur, cut strips of paper and make each one fringed by making small cuts into one of the long edges. Glue the strips onto the piñata so they overlap.

6 Cut out black eyes, brown ears, and a pink nose. Glue them onto the face.

TOP TIP

Start from the tail and work backward.

Fill the piñata with treats and hang it up using string. Take turns bashing the piñata until the treats fall out!

Pet view

Make me my own piñata by putting some treats in a cardboard tube and folding over the ends (see page 23). I'll have fun figuring out how to get in. Remember not to give me anything that has been colored, painted, or glued.

Hamster Facts

5 facts...for hamster lovers

- Humans have kept hamsters as pets for less than 100 years, but the United States is now home to about 1.7 million pet hamsters.

- Could you sniff out your brother or sister in a crowd? Hamsters use their sense of smell to recognize their relatives.

- Hamsters can have up to ten babies at a time, and the babies can have their own babies after just six weeks!

- Like many nocturnal animals, hamsters can't see very well. They explore using their whiskers instead.

- The actress Emma Watson dedicated an acting award to a pet hamster named Millie.

Find out more

FactHound offers a safe, fun way to find Internet sites related to this book. All of the sites on FactHound have been researched by our staff.

Here's all you do:

Visit www.facthound.com

Type in this code: 9781410980670

Templates

Visit **www.capstonepub.com/hip-hamster-projects** and select
"Hip Hamster Projects" to download free templates to use with the
projects in this book. You can also use them to create your own hamster designs.
Once you have printed a template, follow these tips to transfer it to the material
you are working with.

• Use masking tape to hold a sheet of tracing or parchment paper over your
chosen design and draw over the outline with a soft pencil.

• Tape the paper onto the surface you'd like to transfer the picture to.

• Draw over the lines using a pen with a hard point.

Hamster lantern

Hamster pocket pet

BODY
(CUT 2)

NOSE
(CUT 1)

EAR

stitch along
dotted lines

4½ in. (11 cm)

leave gap

Keep out! Door sign

Please say
hello

3 in. (8 cm)

Come back
later

3 in. (8 cm)

TOP TIP

Digital templates are
easy to scale up and
down, so you can
customize the size to
suit your project.

Index